MY FIRST BOOK OF
MAMMALS

by Dee Phillips

MY FIRST BOOK OF
MAMMALS

Copyright © **ticktock Entertainment Ltd 2008**

First published in Great Britain in 2005,

Ticktock Direct Ltd, The Pantiles Chambers, 85 High Street, Tunbridge Wells, Kent, TN1 1XP

ISBN: 978 1 86007 864 4 pbk

Printed in China

10 9 8 7 6

A CIP catalogue record for this book is available from the British Library.

Contents

Words that appear in **bold** are explained in the glossary.

MEET THE MAMMALS

Mammals is a word we use to describe lots of the animals that live on Earth.

The fiercest lion, the biggest elephant and the tallest giraffe are all mammals. It is quite easy to tell if an animal is a mammal:

• Mammals give birth to live babies.

• Mammals feed their babies with milk they make inside their bodies.

• Most mammals have a hairy or furry body.

MAMMAL DIETS

Some mammals, like tigers and seals, only eat meat or fish.
Other mammals, like giraffes and camels, only eat plants.
Many mammals, such as grizzly bears and baboons,
like to eat meat and plants!

Look for these pictures in your book, and they will tell
you what kind of food each animal eats.

Plants

**Meat
(other animals
or bugs)**

Fish

THE WORLD OF MAMMALS

The map on this page shows our world.

The different parts of the world are called continents. North America and Africa are both continents. Some of the animals in this book live in lots of places on just one continent. Other animals live on lots of different continents.

Some animals in this book only live in one country, such as China or Australia.

When you read about an animal in your book, see if you can find the place where they live on the map.

Can you point to the part of the world where you live?

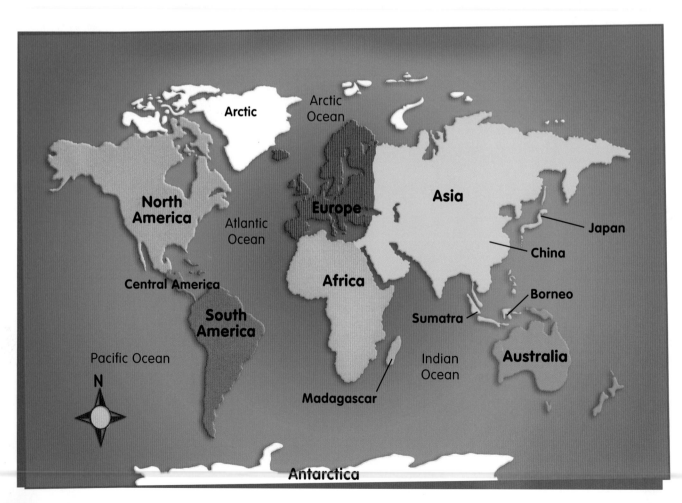

MAMMAL HABITATS

Some animals live in hot places. Others live in cold places. The different types of places where animals live are called **habitats**.

Look for these pictures in your book, and they will tell you what kind of habitat each animal lives in.

Deserts: hot, dry, sandy places where it hardly ever rains

Deciduous forests: forests with trees that lose their leaves in winter

Polar lands: cold, frozen places at the very top and bottom of the Earth

Mountains: high, rocky places

Coniferous forests: cold forests with trees that stay green all year

Grasslands: dry places covered with grass

Lakes, ponds, rivers or streams

Rainforests: warm forests with lots of rain

Oceans: a large part of the sea

ANTEATER

Anteaters live in South America and Central America. Some anteaters live in **forests**. This giant anteater lives on **grasslands**.

Giant anteaters have long snouts for sniffing out ant nests.

The baby anteater rides on its mum's back. Sometimes mum curls her furry tail over the baby to keep it warm.

1m   2m   3m   4m

Anteaters eat ants and **termites**.
They use their sticky tongues to
lap up the tiny bugs.

The giant anteater's tongue is
60 centimetres long!
Anteaters have long,
sharp claws,
but no teeth.

ANTELOPE

Antelope live on the grasslands of Africa and Asia. They can run fast and jump high. Some can even swim!

There are many different kinds of antelope. Some are big and some are small.

An antelope's horns can be long or short, twisted or straight.

This is a kob antelope.

4m

3m

2m

1m

These antelope are springboks.
The baby is called a calf. It drinks milk.
When it grows up, it will eat grass and
leaves like its mother does.

Antelope have hard, tough feet, called
hooves, for running fast.

ARCTIC HARE

Arctic hares live in very cold places in the far north of North America, and the Arctic. They mainly eat grasses, **herbs**, woody plants and **moss**.

Black ear tips

In the winter, the Arctic hare's brown fur turns white. This helps the hare to hide in the snow from **predators**.

A thick, warm coat

1m

2m

Baby hares are called leverets.

Arctic hares can run at 48 kilometres per hour to escape from a predator.

BABOON

Baboons are large **monkeys**. There are five types of baboon. They live in Africa and western Asia, in many different **habitats**.

Baboons live on the ground in large groups called troops.

Baboon babies ride on their mums' backs.

Baboons eat leaves, **roots**, seeds, fruit, birds' eggs, bugs and even lizards!

5m

4m

3m

2m

1m

Male baboons bark to warn the troop if there is danger!

They carry food in their cheek **pouches**.

BEAVER

Beavers are large **rodents**. They live in rivers, streams, **lakes**, ponds and **wetlands** in North America, Europe and Asia.

Baby beavers are called kits or **pups**.

Beavers eat branches, leaves and tree **bark**.

1m

2m

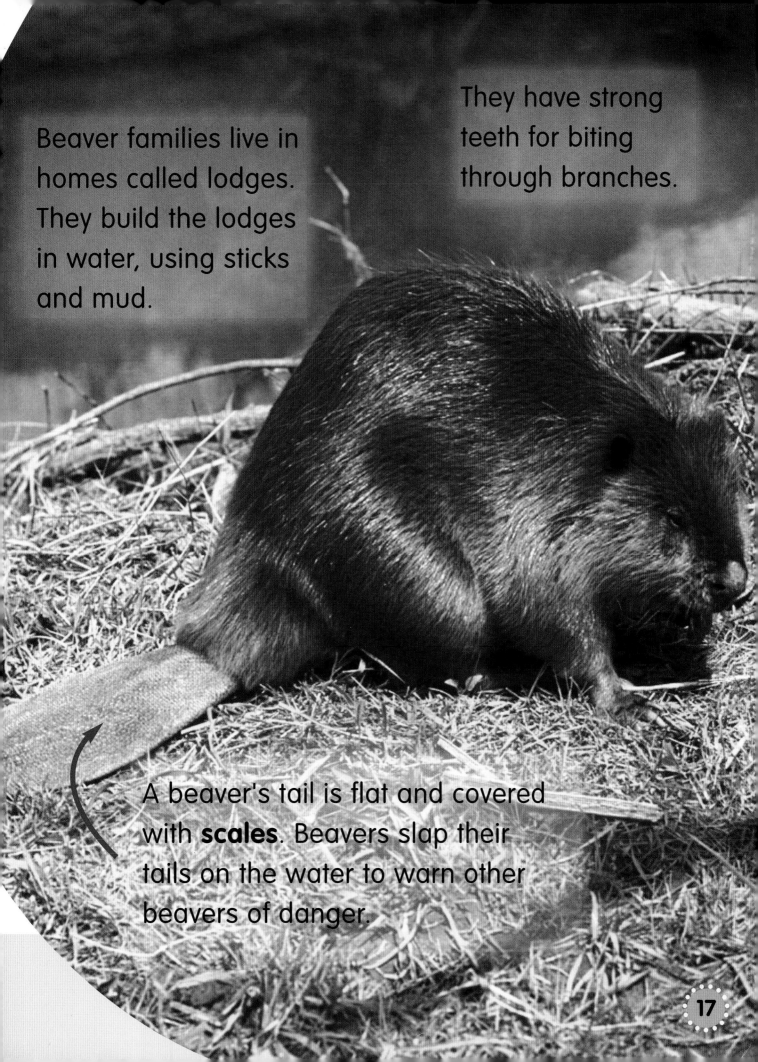

Beaver families live in homes called lodges. They build the lodges in water, using sticks and mud.

They have strong teeth for biting through branches.

A beaver's tail is flat and covered with **scales**. Beavers slap their tails on the water to warn other beavers of danger.

17

BLUE WHALE

Blue whales are the **largest** animals that have ever lived on Earth. They live in all the oceans of the world.

Blue whales make a whistling noise that is louder than a jet plane!

A blue whale's heart is the same size as a small car!

10m   20m   30m   40m

Blue whales eat tiny sea creatures and plants called plankton.

Long, thin flippers

Huge flukes (tail)

A baby blue whale is called a **calf**.

BUFFALO

Buffaloes are big, heavy **mammals**.
They live in hot places in Africa and Asia.

Buffaloes have large horns to protect themselves from **predators**.

They live in huge **herds** on **grasslands**.
Asian buffaloes also live on **wetlands**.
They cool down in pools of water when it gets too hot.

20

Buffaloes eat grass, **herbs** and leaves. They mostly eat at night.

A baby buffalo is called a **calf**. The herd helps the mother buffalo to protect her baby.

CAMEL

Camels live in the **deserts** of Africa and Asia. They live in dry, sandy places where there is very little food or water.

A baby camel is called a **calf**.

Camels eat grass and plants.

There are two types of camels. Bactrian camels have two humps. Dromedaries have one hump.

5m

4m

3m

2m

1m

A camel can go without water for almost two weeks!

Camels store fat in their humps. They use the fat for energy when there is no food.

CHEETAH

Cheetahs live on **grasslands** in Africa and west Asia. They are the *f a s t e s t* of all the land animals!

The cheetah's long legs are good for running.

Cheetahs can run at over 100 kilometres per hour to catch their **prey**!

They hunt and eat antelopes and small, fast animals, like rabbits.

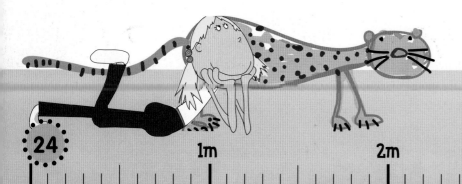

1m   2m   3m   4m

This spotty fur helps the cheetah to hide in long grass and bushes.

Baby cheetahs are called **cubs**. They are blind when they are born.

5m

4m

CHIMPANZEE

Chimpanzees are **apes**. They live in **forests** in Africa. Chimps eat fruit, leaves and bugs – like ants and **termites**.

3m

Chimpanzees walk on all fours. Their arms are longer than their legs.

2m

1m

Chimps make faces to show other chimps that they are happy, frightened or angry!

This baby chimp needs his mum
to do everything for him – just
like you did!

Mother chimps feed,
groom and carry
their babies
around until
the babies
are three
or four
years old.

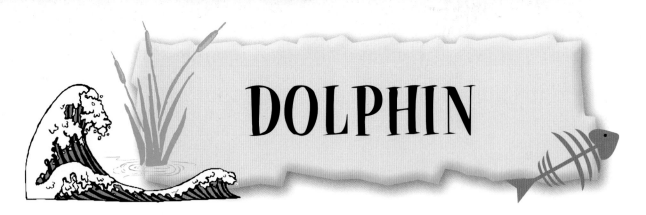

DOLPHIN

Dolphins are **mammals** that live in the ocean and in some rivers. There are many different kinds of dolphin, and they come in lots of sizes!

Dolphins eat fish and **shellfish**.

Dorsal fin

Smooth, rubbery skin

Flipper

A beak with lots of teeth

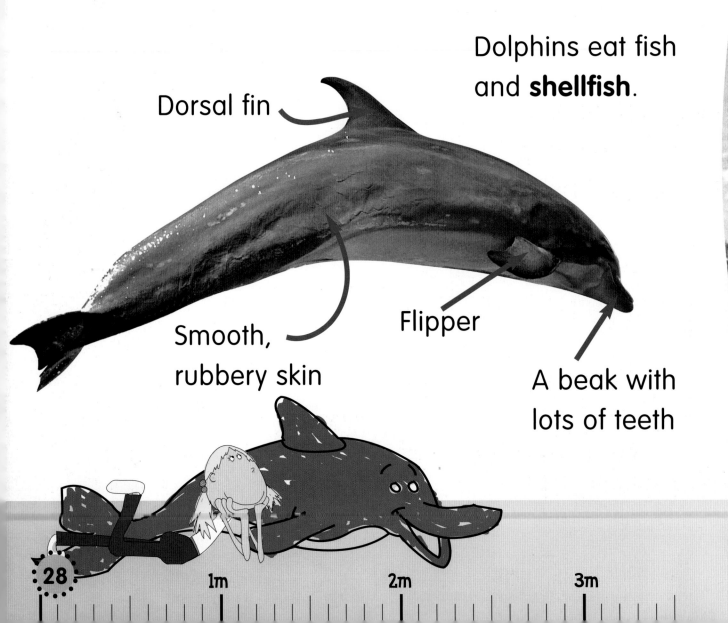

1m   2m   3m

Baby dolphins are called **calves**. They drink milk from their mums under the water.

These bottlenose dolphins can leap six metres into the air!

Dolphins live in groups called pods. They talk to each other using squeaky sounds.

DUCK-BILLED PLATYPUS

Duck-billed platypuses live in ponds and small rivers in Australia. They eat **shellfish**, worms, bugs and snails.

Duck-billed platypuses are very unusual **mammals** because they lay eggs!

When the eggs **hatch**, the mother platypus feeds milk to the babies. Baby platypuses are called puggles.

1m   2m

Duck-billed platypuses live in **burrows** dug into riverbanks.

They have a flat mouth, shaped like a duck's beak.

They have **waterproof** fur and **webbed** feet for swimming.

ELEPHANT

Elephants live in Africa and Asia. They are the **biggest** animals that live on land.

Female elephants live in **herds** with their babies. Male elephants live on their own.

A baby elephant is called a **calf**. Calves weigh over 100 kilograms when they are born!

2m   4m   6m   8m

Elephants eat grass, leaves, **roots**, branches, **bark** and fruit.

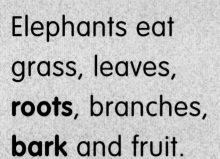

They drink enough water to fill a bathtub, every day!

Elephants use their trunks for smelling, picking up food and sucking up water.

These HUGE teeth are called **tusks**.

FRUIT BAT

Bats are **mammals** that fly! There are many different types, including lots of different fruit bats.

Fruit bats live in **forests** in Africa, Europe, Asia and Australia.

A baby bat is called a **pup**.

Fruit bats come in lots of sizes.

1m   2m   3m   4m

Fruit bats only eat the juice and the soft, squishy parts of fruit.

The bat's wings fold up.

This is a flying fox fruit bat.

They search for food at night. During the day they rest, hanging upside down!

GIANT PANDA

Giant pandas live in just one small part of China, in Asia. They live high in the **mountains** in cold, wet **forests**.

Pandas eat bamboo – a tough, woody grass. They hold it in their front paws.

Pandas need to eat lots of bamboo to get all the energy they need. So they eat for up to 12 hours every day.

5m

4m

3m

2m

1m

A baby panda is called a **cub**.

Cubs are blind, hairless and just 15 centimetres long when they are born.

GIRAFFE

Giraffes are the **tallest** animals in the world. They live on **grasslands** in Africa.

Giraffes eat leaves and twigs.

A giraffe's long neck and tongue help it reach leaves at the tops of trees. A giraffe's tongue can be 45 centimetres long!

5m

4m

3m

2m

1m

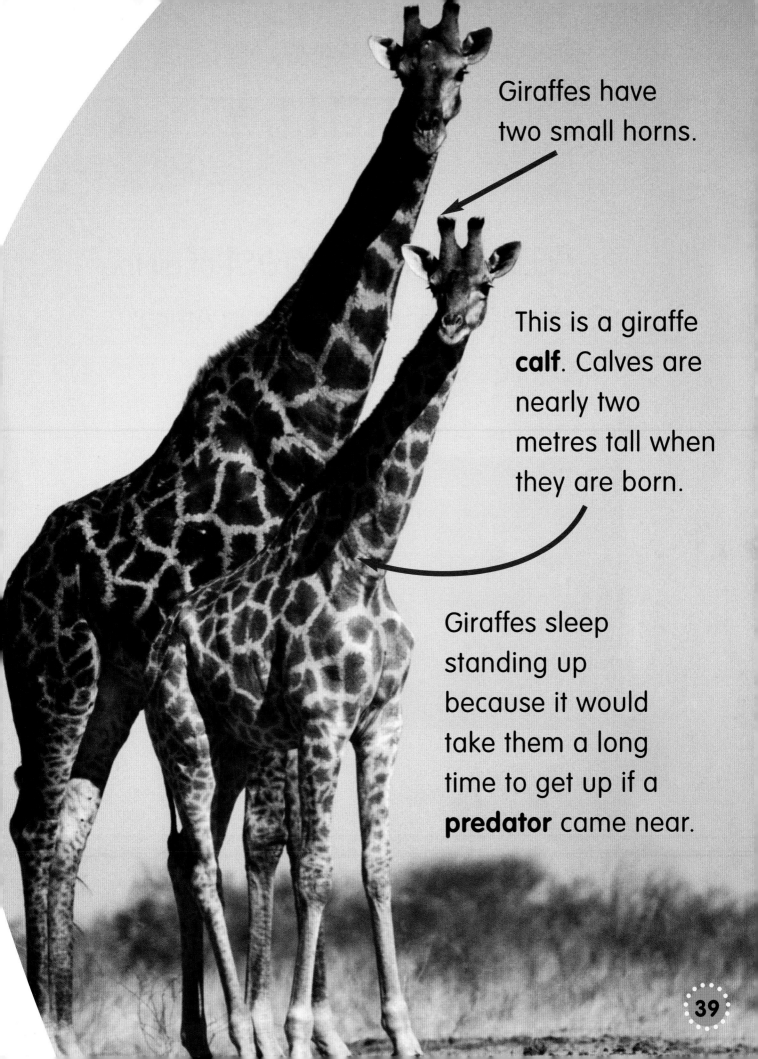

Giraffes have two small horns.

This is a giraffe **calf**. Calves are nearly two metres tall when they are born.

Giraffes sleep standing up because it would take them a long time to get up if a **predator** came near.

GORILLA

Gorillas are the **biggest** of all the **apes**. They live in **forests** in Africa. Gorillas eat plants and fruit.

Grown-up male gorillas have silver-coloured fur on their backs. They are called silverbacks.

5m

4m

3m

2m

1m

Gorillas live in family groups. The silverback is the leader of the family.

Grown-up gorillas teach the babies how to find food.

At night, gorillas build nests of branches and leaves to sleep in.

Gorillas are gentle and very clever. Baby gorillas like to play!

GRIZZLY BEAR

Bears are big, heavy **mammals**, with thick, hairy coats. Grizzly bears live in **mountains** and **forests** in some parts of North America.

Baby bears are called **cubs**. They live with their mothers until they are three or four years old.

Grizzly bears eat plants, meat and sometimes fish.

1m   2m   3m

Bears have large, long snouts that help them sniff out food.

Grizzly bears spend the cold winter months sleeping in cosy **dens**, caves or **hollow** logs.

HIPPOPOTAMUS

Hippopotamuses live in lakes, rivers and **wetlands** in Africa. They have huge mouths and teeth, and can be very fierce.

Baby hippos are born underwater and can weigh up to 50 kilograms.

A baby hippo is called a **calf**.

1m   2m   3m

A hippo can close its nostrils so water cannot get in!

Hippos live in **herds**.

Hippos spend most of the day in the water. At night they come out onto land to eat grass.

KANGAROO

Kangaroos live on **grasslands** and in **forests** in Australia.

Kangaroos hop very fast using their big, strong back legs.

Their tails help them to balance.

A baby kangaroo is only two centimetres long when it is born. It lives and grows in its mum's special **pouch**. Animals that do this are called **marsupials**.

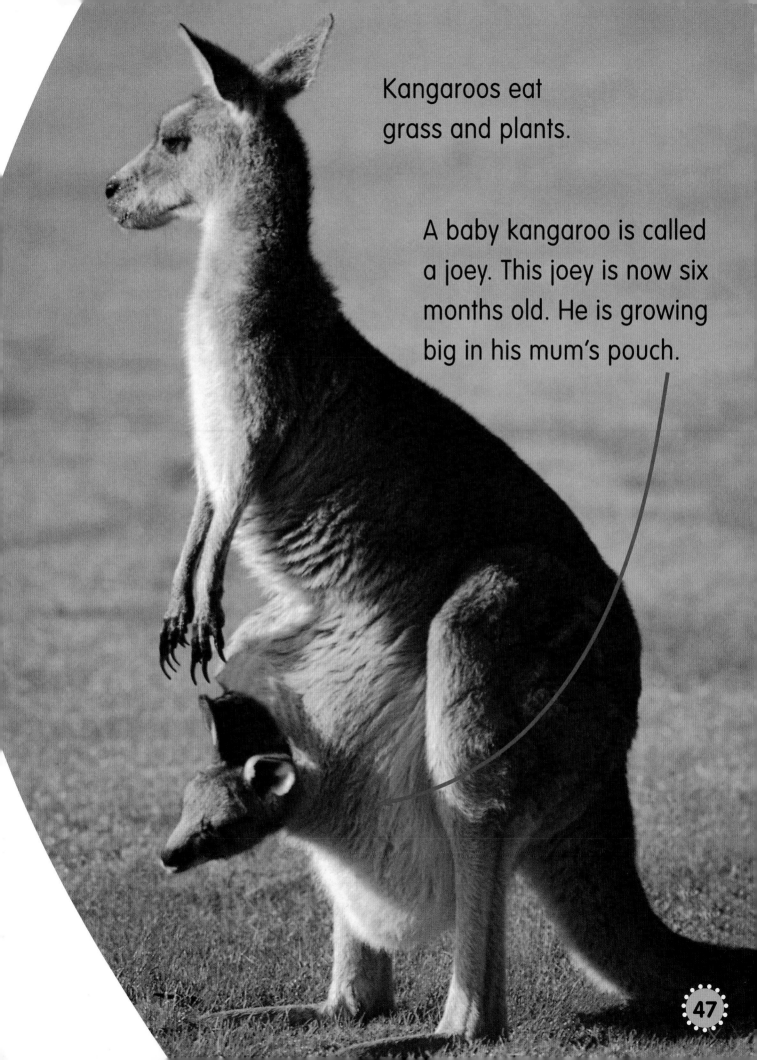

Kangaroos eat
grass and plants.

A baby kangaroo is called
a joey. This joey is now six
months old. He is growing
big in his mum's pouch.

KOALA

Koalas live in Australia. They live in eucalyptus trees and eat eucalyptus leaves. Koalas are **marsupials**.

Baby koalas are called joeys.

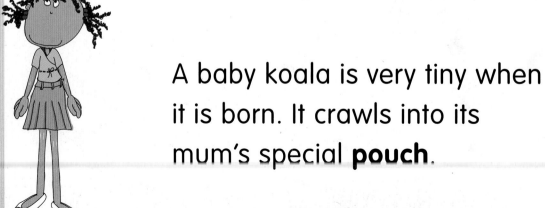

A baby koala is very tiny when it is born. It crawls into its mum's special **pouch**.

5m

4m

3m

2m

1m

Koalas sleep for up to 20 hours each day!

This thick, woolly coat protects the koala from rain and cold.

Koalas have claws and rough pads on their feet for holding onto branches.

49

LEMUR

Lemurs are part of the same animal family as **monkeys** and **apes**.

This ring-tailed lemur lives on Madagascar, an island near Africa.

Black and white tail rings.

Ring-tailed lemurs live on the ground and in trees.

Baby lemurs hold tightly onto their mum's back as she leaps through the trees.

1m

2m

Ring-tailed lemurs like to sunbathe!

Ring-tailed lemurs eat fruit, plants, birds' eggs and small animals like frogs.

51

LEOPARD

Leopards are big cats. They live on **grasslands** and in **deserts**, and **forests** in Africa and Asia.

Baby leopards are called **cubs**. They live with their mums until they are about two years old.

Grown-up leopards live on their own.

1m   2m   3m

Leopards hunt many different animals, from birds and baboons to big antelopes.

Leopards are very good at climbing. They hide their food up in trees.

LION

Lions are big, strong cats. They live in family groups called prides. These African lions live on **grasslands**.

The male lion has a thick, furry mane.

Females are called lionesses.

A male lion's **ROAR** can be heard eight kilometres away.

1m   2m   3m

Lions eat antelopes, buffaloes and zebras. Groups of lionesses hunt as a team!

This is a lion **cub**. All the lionesses in a pride help to look after each other's cubs.

MANDRILL

Mandrills are the **biggest** members of the **monkey** family. They live in **forests** in Africa.

This baby mandrill holds on to his mum's tummy. When he gets heavier, he will ride on her back.

Mandrills eat seeds, fruit, birds' eggs and small animals. They carry extra food in their cheek **pouches**.

5m

4m

3m

2m

1m

Mandrill families spend all day searching for food on the ground. At night, they sleep in trees.

Male mandrills have red and blue faces.

MEERKAT

Meerkats live on **grasslands** in Africa. They live in big groups in underground **burrows**.

Baby meerkats are called **pups**.

One grown-up meerkat babysits all the pups when the rest of the group goes to look for food.

Meerkat look-outs stand on high places and make a special noise if they see a **predator**.

Meerkats eat bugs, plants and small animals such as lizards and mice.

They have long claws for digging burrows and digging up bugs.

MOOSE

Moose live in **forests** in North America, Europe and Asia. They are the **biggest** of all the **deer**.

A baby moose is called a **calf**.

Moose eat twigs and **bark** in the winter. In the summer, they paddle around in lakes eating water plants.

5m
4m
3m
2m
1m

Moose are fast runners and very good swimmers.

The antlers fall off every year and then grow back.

A male moose has huge **antlers**, which can grow to 1.5 metres long!

ORANGUTAN

Orangutans live in **forests** in Borneo and Sumatra, in Asia. They are the **largest** tree-living animal in the world.

Baby orangutans are carried by their mums until they are about three years old.

They have long arms for climbing and swinging.

Orangutans mainly eat fruit. Mums chew it up to make it soft for their babies.

5m

4m

3m

2m

1 m

Male orangutans have large, soft cheek pads. They feel like leather!

Clever orangutans use leaves as umbrellas when it rains.

ORCA

Orcas are a kind of whale. They live in all the world's oceans. Orcas can swim at 48 kilometres per hour to catch their **prey**.

Orcas live in big family groups called pods. Baby orcas are called **calves**.

Calves stay with their mums their whole lives.

This dorsal fin can be 1.8 metres tall.

Thick **blubber** keeps the orca warm in icy water.

Orcas are very good hunters. They eat fish, birds, seals and even sharks!

OTTER

Otters live in rivers and **lakes** all over the world. Sea otters live in the sea.

Otters mainly eat fish and **shellfish**. Sea otters crack open shellfish by BASHING them with rocks!

Baby otters are called **cubs** or **pups**. Otter families love to chase each other and play together.

1m   2m

Otters are very good swimmers. They have **waterproof** fur and **webbed** feet.

The sea otter has the thickest fur of any animal in the world!

POLAR BEAR

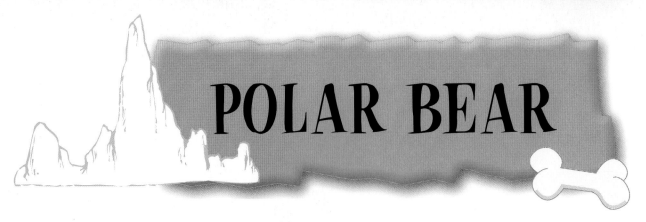

Polar bears live in the Arctic on icy, cold land and on huge areas of frozen ocean.

A baby polar bear is called a **cub**. Mother polar bears dig **dens** in the snow, where they give birth to their cubs.

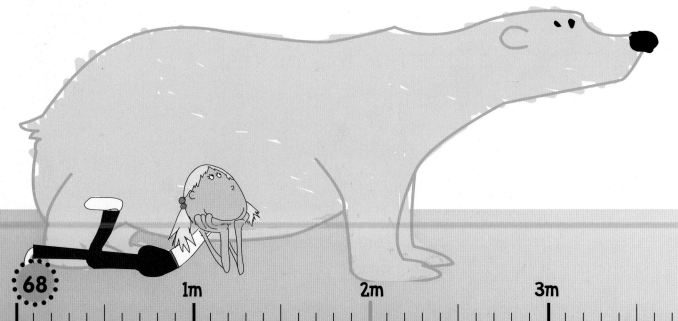

1m   2m   3m   4m

Polar bears
are the biggest
predator that
lives on land.
Their main food
is seals.

Polar bears can
smell food from
32 kilometres away!

They have thick
fur and **blubber**.

Their huge paws
are the size of
dinner plates!

69

PORCUPINE

Porcupines live in North America, South America and Africa. They are covered in spikes called quills. Baby porcupines are called porcupettes.

The quills protect the porcupine from **predators**.

African porcupines make their homes in piles of rocks or in small caves.

Porcupines' teeth never stop growing! They chew on foods like **bark** to wear them down.

Porcupines mainly eat plants, **roots**, fruit, berries and nuts.

North American porcupines climb trees to look for food.

RACCOON

Raccoons live in many different **habitats** in North America. They eat bugs, nuts, berries, frogs – lots of different foods!

A baby raccoon is called a kit.

Raccoons sometimes steal leftovers from dustbins! If food is dirty, they wash it in water.

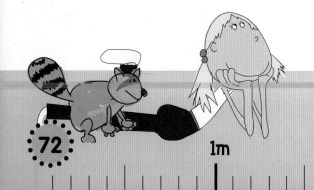

1m   2m   3m   4

Raccoons have a bushy, stripey tail.

Cheeky raccoons can use their little hands to open door latches, turn on taps and even open cans of fizzy drink!

REINDEER

Reindeer are a type of **deer**. They live in **forests** and in snowy, icy places at the far north of North America, Europe and Asia.

Reindeer live in big **herds**. A baby reindeer is called a **calf**.

In the winter, reindeer dig in the snow with their hooves to find **moss** to eat.

1m   2m   3m

In the summer, reindeer eat grass and **herbs**.

Male and female reindeer have **antlers**.

Reindeer have thick brown fur to keep them warm.

75

RHINOCEROS

Rhinos are HUGE **mammals**. They live in **forests** and on **grasslands** in Africa and Asia. Rhinos eat grasses and plants.

There are five different kinds of rhino. The rhinos in this picture are white rhinos. They can weigh over two tonnes.

A baby rhinoceros is called a **calf**. Its mum uses her horn to protect her calf from **predators**.

1m   2m   3m   4m

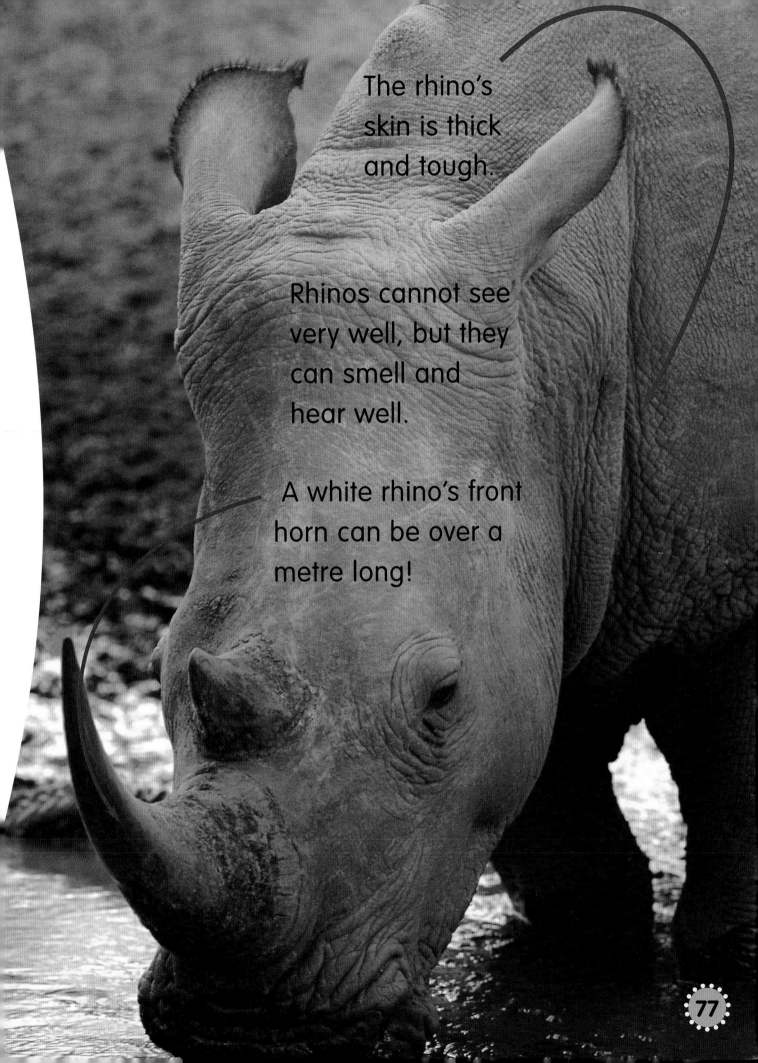

The rhino's skin is thick and tough.

Rhinos cannot see very well, but they can smell and hear well.

A white rhino's front horn can be over a metre long!

SEAL

There are many different kinds of seal.

They live in oceans all over the world.

Seals mainly eat fish and squid.

A baby seal is called a **pup**. Seals give birth to their pups on beaches, rocks, or on huge chunks of floating ice.

This harp seal pup has white fur so **predators** cannot see him on the ice.

1m   2m   3m

Seals are clumsy on land, but they are very good swimmers and divers.

This is a grey seal.

SNOW MONKEY

These furry **monkeys** live in **forests** and on **mountains** in Japan, in Asia.

In the cold winter, some snow monkeys warm up by sitting in pools of hot water. Warmth from under the ground makes the water hot.

Snow monkeys eat leaves and flowers, **bark** and fruit. Sometimes they eat crabs and grasshoppers.

5m
4m
3m
2m
1 m

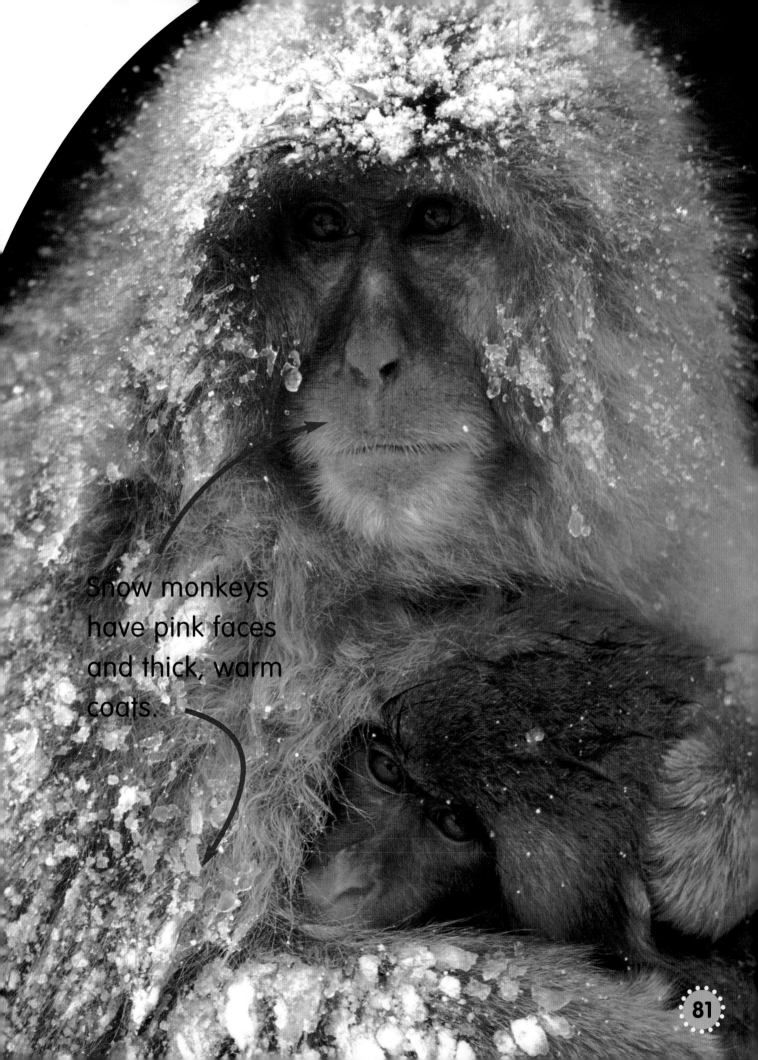

Snow monkeys have pink faces and thick, warm coats.

TAMARIN

Tamarins are small **monkeys**.

They live in **forests** in South America.

Tamarins live in small family groups high in the treetops.

The group take it in turn to carry the babies around, to give their mums a rest.

1m   2m   3m   4m

This is a golden lion tamarin. Its silky mane makes it look like a little lion!

Golden lion tamarins eat bugs, fruit and small lizards.

Most monkeys have fingernails, but tamarins have little claws.

TIGER

Tigers are the **biggest** members of the cat family. They live in **forests** in Asia. Grown-up tigers normally live alone.

Tigers mainly hunt at night. They can catch big animals such as **deer** and antelopes.

Baby tigers are called **cubs**.

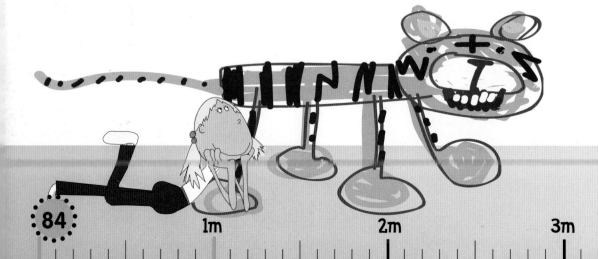

1m   2m   3m

Some tigers live in hot places. They like to go swimming to keep cool. Other tigers live in cold, snowy places.

Tigers have black stripes. Every tiger's stripey pattern is different.

WALRUS

Walruses are huge, heavy **mammals**.
They live in the Arctic, on land and in the sea.

Walruses can stay underwater for
25 minutes, searching for **shellfish**
and sea-snails.

A baby walrus
is called a **calf**.
This big baby
weighed
75 kilograms
when it was born!

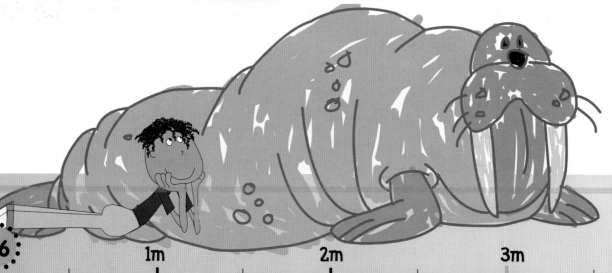

1m   2m   3m   4m

A grown-up male's **tusks** can be up to one metre long!

Walruses have thick, crumpled skin.

Big groups of hundreds of walruses often lie together on beaches or chunks of floating ice.

WARTHOG

Warthogs are fast-running wild pigs.

They live on **grasslands** in Africa.

At night, warthogs sleep in **burrows**.

Baby warthogs are called piglets. Mums have three or four piglets at one time.

When it's hot, warthogs cool off by taking mud baths.

1m   2m   3m   4m

Warthogs eat grass, berries, **bark**, and sometimes dead animals!

They dig for food using their strong snouts.

These **tusks** can be 60 centimetres long!

89

WOLF

Wolves live in **forests** in North America, Europe and Asia. They live in small family groups called packs.

A baby wolf is called a **pup** or **cub**. Normally four to seven pups are born at once in a cosy **den**.

Wolf families howl together. This tells other wolves not to come near the family's home area.

1m   2m   3m

Wolf packs hunt big animals like reindeer.

Thick fur keeps the wolf warm.

Long, sharp teeth and a good sense of smell make the wolf a good hunter.

ZEBRA

Zebras are wild cousins of horses. They live on **grasslands** in Africa, and their main food is grass.

A baby zebra is called a foal. The foal can stand up just a few minutes after it is born!

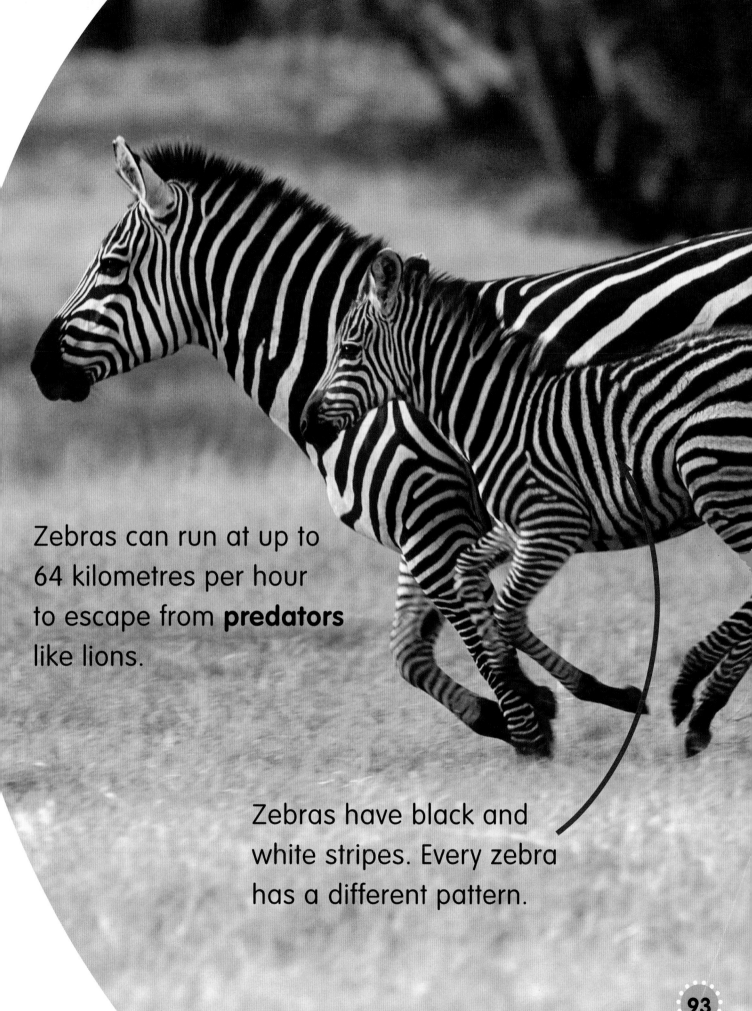

Zebras can run at up to
64 kilometres per hour
to escape from **predators**
like lions.

Zebras have black and
white stripes. Every zebra
has a different pattern.

Glossary

antlers Horn-like growths on the heads of deer.

apes Animals from the primate family (which includes monkeys, humans and lemurs). Apes and monkeys look a bit alike, but while most monkeys have tails, apes don't.

bark The tough, outer covering of tree trunks and branches.

blubber A thick layer of fat under the skin.

burrows Holes or tunnels that animals dig as homes.

calf (calves) The name for the babies of antelopes, buffaloes, whales, camels, dolphins, elephants, giraffes, hippos, deer, rhinos and walruses.

cubs The name for the babies of cheetahs, giant pandas, grizzly bears, leopards, lions, otters, polar bears, tigers and wolves.

deer A family of plant-eating animals. The males normally have antlers.

dens The homes of wild animals.

deserts Hot, dry places where hardly any rain falls. Only a few plants and animals live in deserts.

forests Places where there are lots of trees. Coniferous forests are cold, with trees that never lose their leaves. Rainforests are warm, jungle-like forests.

grasslands Dry places covered with grass, and very few bushes or trees.

groom When an animal cleans itself and takes care of its fur or hair.

habitats Different types of places around the world, such as forests, deserts and grasslands.

hatch To be born by breaking out of an egg.

herbs Plants that have a strong smell and taste. People use herbs for cooking.

herds Large groups of animals.

hollow Something that is empty inside.

lakes Large areas of water surrounded by land.

mammals Animals with fur or hair that give birth to live babies and feed them milk.

marsupials Mammals that carry their newborn babies in a pouch until the babies are big enough to look after themselves.

monkeys Animals from the primate family (which includes apes, humans and lemurs). Monkeys and apes look a bit alike, but while most monkeys have tails, apes don't.

moss Tiny, low-growing, bushy plants that spread over rocks or logs.

mountains Large, rocky areas of land that are much higher than the land around them.

pouch (pouches) A kind of pocket, made of skin, on the front of a marsupial animal; also a place for storing food inside an animal's cheeks.

predators Animals that live by hunting and eating other animals.

prey An animal that is hunted by another animal for food.

pups The name for the babies of beavers, bats, meerkats, seals and wolves.

rodents A group of animals that gnaw a lot. The group includes beavers and mice.

roots The part of a plant that is under the ground.

scales Tough, flat sections of skin on the tails of beavers, and on the bodies of animals such as fish and snakes.

shellfish Water animals with bodies covered in a shell, such as prawns.

termites Small bugs that live in huge colonies (groups). They build mountain-shaped nests.

tusks Long, pointed teeth that grow out of an animal's face or mouth.

waterproof Something that does not let water in.

webbed Feet where the toes are joined by flaps of skin to help with swimming.

wetlands Places where there is lots of water, such as ponds and streams, and where water plants grow.

Index

Picture credits

We would like to thank Ardea, Corbis, FLPA and Oxford Scientific Photo Library for the images used in this book.